# D**o**gs

# Dogs

# Dogs
# in the
# Animal World

The large grey wolf has exceptional sensory faculties: it has very sharp eyesight, a keen ear and a very highly developed sense of smell.

# Dogs, wolves and their cousins

*Dogs, wolves, jackals and coyotes have spread across every part of the world except the icy polar regions. Tireless runners with a predatory instinct, all these canine cousins have the same tastes: they are carnivorous.*

Three dingoes make some friendly overtures before taking a short siesta. The other members of the pack gnaw at a marsupial carcass.

The wolf's coat varies in colour from region to region.

There are around 350 breeds of dog, making up one species: *Canis familiaris*. According to the latest studies, all these breeds are the result of domesticating the wolf. Dogs are not simply tame wolves, however; partly because they have acquired physical and behavioural features that distinguish them from their wild cousins, and partly because they were probably crossbred with other canines such as the jackal.

In a pack, the wolf adopts a posture in keeping with its place in the hierarchy. The submissive members stretch out before the dominant ones, with their tails between their hind legs.

The she-wolf is always vigilant and alert, and does not risk lying down to feed her hungry cubs.

## A wolf lies dormant in every dog

The oldest fossils that we can be sure came from the skeleton of a domestic canine were discovered in Iran, in 14,000-year-old geological strata. At that time, two great predators shared the same territory: human beings and wolves. Although they hunted the same prey, the two groups seemed to tolerate each other, each one benefiting from the presence of the other. For

Frightening! An angry wolf is a very dangerous animal.

example, when a wolf howled to signal danger to the pack, people would recognize the warning and take shelter. In return, the wolves would spend their nights close to the human camps, where the firelight protected them from the big cats. They also feasted on the carcasses that people left them. It did not take the bipeds long to see the potential to turn their four-legged counterparts into guards. They tried to tame them, captured their first wolf cubs, and, since the ways of life and social organizations of the two groups were relatively similar, the operation proved successful. People then began to control the reproduction of their animals and launched a process of selective breeding to obtain descendants that were more docile, and suitable for defence, for guiding their flocks, or for hunting.

A good night's sleep in the shelter of a rocky crevice.

## The jackal family, from Africa to Asia

At ease wherever they go, golden jackals are common from North Africa to Thailand, including south-eastern Europe and the Middle East. Golden jackals operate in couples to defend their hunting grounds.

Wolves are tireless walkers and continually roam their territory in pairs, seeking potential game.

Wolves are capable of producing a wide range of sounds, including several different varieties of howl, which enable them to synchronize the movements of the pack, and also to announce their presence to other animals. Dogs, who lost their packs long ago, have relegated howling to a much more minor role. On the other hand, they have now become fluent at barking. They bark to express hunger or fear, to point out danger, or simply to give their owners a joyful greeting.

The size of each couple's territory depends on the amount of available game. Their cubs, usually five or six in number, rarely leave the den during their first few weeks. Outside, they may be exposed to the deadly beak of an eagle. When they are 30 to 40 days old they accompany their parents on their first hunt, making clumsy attempts to capture small mammals, lizards and insects. At four months, when they are not yet fully grown, they try out their first hunting ruses. By far the most

The common jackal proudly sports large ears commensurate with its sense of hearing.

The jackal often has to fight with vultures for its meals. The large birds are fearless and the competition around a carcass is fierce.

The jackal is opportunistic and will eat ostrich eggs. Its pointed canine teeth bite easily through the tough shell of this very nourishing dish.

Nibbling is usually a sign of affection in canids.

effective trick is to play dead until some prey becomes too curious.

## The Ethiopian wolf (or Simien jackal): the most discreet member of the family

Long high-pitched howls in the rugged Ethiopian Hills announce the presence of the Ethiopian wolf. There are only an estimated 1000 of these animals, isolated at altitudes between 3000 and 4000 metres. This rare

Although the coyote has a bloodcurdling, piercing howl, it is very reserved by nature. A well-positioned rocky overhang provides an effective means of camouflage.

 breed remains an unknown quantity to scientists, who are uncertain whether it is more closely related to the fox, the jackal or the wolf. As long as it can find plenty of rabbits, with the occasional antelope carcass on the menu, this wolf-like creature has a chance of survival.

## The coyote, an American cousin

When the first settlers set foot in North America they discovered

The ever-alert coyote surveys its territory from on high.

The extremely timid coyote's fawn and beige coat means that it can blend into its surroundings.

In dingo families, the young play the same games and have the same bearing as their cousin the domestic dog.

The dingo is so similar to the dog that it is hard to tell them apart.

an animal that howled at the moon when evening fell. It was immediately christened 'howling wolf'. Since that time coyotes have had a price on their heads: they made the mistake of developing a taste for mutton and chicken, as well as being carriers of rabies. Although they have been destroyed systematically, coyotes have benefited from the increasing scarcity of wolves and actually extended their territory, which now stretches from Alaska to southern Mexico.

## The dingo, a rebel in Australian exile

The dingo is the dog's closest relative. In fact, it appears to be the dog's twin brother who returned to the wild. When the Aborigines arrived in Australia several thousand years ago, the dogs that they had brought with them took advantage of the immense wide-open spaces and escaped from their masters.

The dingo's curiosity means that it often forgets to be wary.

Due to its genetic make-up or cross-breeding with a stray dog, the dingo's coat can vary in colour even though the dominant fawn colour is still evident.

The alsatian, which is no longer used as a sheepdog, is universally loved. It is found everywhere, in all climates and in all sorts of positions.

# Sheepdogs keep careful watch

*Sheepdogs are the result of selective breeding carried out by people in ancient times. These dogs have a lively and often boisterous nature and have acquired exceptional powers of physical endurance. They need to be ruled with a firm hand, and really come into their own in wide-open spaces.*

The Bouvier des Flandres was extremely useful for taking herds of cattle to the abattoir, but it almost became extinct during World War I.

Sheepdogs are invaluable assistants, fulfilling two very important functions in rural life: they guide the flocks to the pastures, and protect them from wild animals and from dishonest people. Selectively bred to carry out this demanding work, these intelligent dogs have developed exceptional abilities over the centuries. Nowadays they can be trained to do many different types of work.

The Canaan dog is the most popular sheepdog in Israel.

The colour and length of the alsatian's coat can vary: it can be very short or very long, and very dark or very light.

The bobtail derived its name from the fact that the English used to dock their working dogs' tails.

The border collie's ancestors may have arrived in Scotland with the Vikings.

## Sheepdog: a job requiring many skills

The mastiffs of central Asia were the first dogs to go into service with shepherds. These powerful, heavy, tough animals had the perfect physical characteristics and the right blend of courage, intelligence and aggressiveness for defending livestock against bears and wolves. Over the ages they grew lighter, resulting in a breed of dog that was quicker and even more resilient.

The bearded collie's dense beard and long hair are an effective protection again the cold during the very damp winters in the Scottish Highlands.

▼ Faced with a flock, sheepdogs begin to behave instinctively like predators. In their case these reflex actions are not caused by hunger, but by playfulness and the pleasure associated with hunting. They are used to living with people, who they very soon took to be the leaders of their packs, and they are trained to content themselves with feigning attacks on their keeper's animals. They herd and round up livestock by adapting their runs according to the reactions of the flock.

Today's sheepdogs can be divided into two groups, according to their main abilities. The first group consists of the dogs most suited to defending the flock. They have stocky bodies and light coats. They are virtually fearless, and on no account will they leave their livestock unattended. In the second group are the dogs whose main role is to guide the flocks. They are quicker and brighter than the dogs in the first group, and they herd goats and sheep by mimicking hunting postures.

The laekenois is a Belgian sheepdog, identifiable by its rough, fawn-coloured coat.

## The German shepherd

The Alsatian is now the most common dog in the world. However, the breed only appeared at the end of the 19th century, when the Prussian officer Max von Stephanitz carried out a rigorous selective breeding process after crossing different breeds of sheepdog. The Alsatian's black and tawny coat, its slender yet powerful physique, its long head, piercingly bright eyes and large, erect ears give it a falsely wolf-like appearance. Apart from their exceptional physical abilities, these dogs are renowned for their psycho-

The Catalan sheepdog is at home in the mountains and is fond of slopes.

logical qualities. They are said to be very brave, and their courage is reinforced by a strong fighting instinct, or even aggressiveness, which is fortunately kept in check by nerves of steel. Their loyalty and aptitude for training make them valued companions.

## The Welsh 'fox-dog'

The ancestors of the Cardigan Welsh corgi probably appeared in the hills of Wales

The Cardigan Welsh corgi is easily identifiable by its short legs. It is distinguished from its cousin the Pembroke by its bushy tail resembling that of a fox.

The alsatian was bred to round up flocks, but these days it performs many tasks. Its physical qualities make it an acrobat without equal!

The Beauceron's powerful mouth makes it an excellent guard dog for flocks, and its size also adds to its impressive air.

The Australian shepherd has only very distant Australian origins. It was widely imported to the West Coast of the United States and the breed's standards were set in America.

The Anatolian shepherd, a descendant of the mastiff, keeps wolves at bay.

3000 years ago, when the Celts migrated there. While Alsatians bear a resemblance to their cousins the wolves, corgis are more like that other famous member of the canine family, the fox. Physically, these short-legged dogs are uncannily close to foxes: they have the same bushy tails, triangular heads and large pointed ears. Measuring 30 centimetres at the shoulder, corgis are more comfortable herding sheep (or the royal family in Buckingham Palace) than rounding up cattle.

The four breeds of the famous Belgian sheepdogs are (from left to right), the tervuren, the groenendael, the malinois and the laekenois.

They are tireless workers who perform their tasks in a lively and cheerful way, and even indulge in a little clowning.

## The puli, dreadlocks in Hungary

Pulis are the descendants of sheepdogs that were brought to the Great Hungarian Plain by the Magyars when they settled in Hungary in the ninth century. These resilient dogs, whose

There are no insurmountable obstacles for the alsatian.

name means leader in Hungarian, guard large flocks of sheep, but only during the day. At night their dark coats make it hard for them to attract the attention of the sheep. Pulis have solidly-built, muscular bodies and a coat resembling dreadlocks. Loyal – to the point of being intrusive – and intelligent, they show great bravery around their owners, and are sometimes hostile towards strangers.

The Briard is a country animal and needs to let off steam.

The puli, which is protected by its abundant mane, never hesitates to take the plunge; its owner can then spend time washing and disentangling its coat.

## The collie, a gentleman farmer in the Highlands

The collie is the result of a mysterious breeding process, from uncertain origins, that aimed to produce a dog suited to the harsh climate of northern Scotland. Its very name is surrounded by legends. Some people claim that it comes from a breed of sheep called 'collies' that were only herded by these dogs. Others believe that the origin of the name comes from 'collar', for this elegant animal's coat has a collar of white fur. Quick and obedient, these dogs can sometimes be timid, and are renowned for their self-control and sense of humour, according to the British, anyway.

In Italy, the Maremma sheepdog confronts wolves.

## An Italian giant against the wolves

The Italian Maremma and Abruzzi sheepdog is the archetypal guard dog bred to protect livestock. They are large dogs, and have inherited great physical strength from their ancestors. Their pale coats make it easy to distinguish them from their enemy, the wolf. They are calm, docile dogs, but can turn ferocious when they need to protect their flocks.

The long-haired collie is the most common of the collie breeds. Although a popular house dog among town and city dwellers, it is not ideally suited to an indoor life.

▼ Carnivorous by nature, with predatory instincts, dogs in pursuit of other animals can get carried away and become dangerous. Stray dogs, so used to being around people that they do not fear them, think nothing of attacking flocks of sheep. These savage hunting parties, which are not always motivated by the need for food, cause far more losses among livestock than the levies taken by wolves. To fend off these murderous attacks, farmers turn to big strong sheepdogs.

The enormous chops of the Neapolitan mastiff make it look deceptively easy-going. When threatened, however, its violent mastiff origins come to the fore.

# From the mastiff to the husky

To protect their belongings, human beings call on the guarding instinct of the dog. At first they produced powerful mastiffs for this purpose, then breeds such as pinschers and schnauzers that were quicker and more alert. In cold regions the big all-purpose dogs ended up pulling sledges.

The Norwegian elkhound can trace its roots back to the Viking era. This nordic dog can, when necessary, pull a sleigh.

S chnauzers and pinchers can come from any of around ten different breeds of dog which all have their origins in Germany. The stubborn nature of these animals, hardened by a tough training programme, makes them exceptional guard dogs.

## The dwarf pinscher, the smallest dog to beware of

The scaled-down model of the group is a miniature replica of the regular pinscher. It was first

The pinscher, with its fine sense of hearing and loud bark, makes a good guard dog.

The affenpinscher, which means 'monkey pinscher' in German, owes its name to the long hair around its face, giving it a monkey-like look.

A canine colossus, the giant schnauzer often reaches heights of 70 centimetres at the shoulder. They are bad-tempered dogs and hardly stand the company of their own kind.

The dwarf pinscher, which was bred to hunt rats, has a nasty bite.

shown officially at the Stuttgart dog show in 1900 and was a great success, at first with American breeders, then later with Europeans. Its popularity was undoubtedly due to its small stature, perfectly suited to apartment life, and to its truculent character. Brimming with affection towards their owners, to the point of jealousy, these dogs can be bad tempered, even downright nasty to strangers. They need a lot of exercise and strict training to keep their highly-strung nerves in check.

# Doberman, the ultimate pinscher

According to dog clubs, the doberman was created in the German region of Thuringia by L. Doberman, who was in charge of the dog pound at the time. Its ancestors include the pinscher, the German mastiff, the beauceron and the black and tan terrier. Dominant by nature, dobermans make excellent guard dogs.

The dobermann can be a ferocious bodyguard.

## The many versions of the schnauzer

Albrecht Dürer painted one in 1492, but the origins of the schnauzer go much further back than that. They were highly valued as ratters at the time, then later became faithful stagecoach guards. They would caper alongside the horses on stagecoach journeys, or go on scouting excursions to explore the road ahead. At night in the coaching inns they kept watch at their masters' side. These dogs were especially well loved in Württemberg, their native region, where breeders developed miniature dogs such as the dwarf schnauzer, and big dogs like the giant schnauzer.

The German mastiff, despite its imposing stature, is very gentle with children. Kids love the clumsy appearance of this living toy.

▼ The Epirus molosse, an immigrant in Britain, was one of the ancestors of the bulldog. Once it had arrived in the British Isles, its new keepers strove to bring out its physical anomalies, producing a short-legged, stocky dog with a sullen expression. In the 18th and 19th centuries these dogs were bred for power and aggressiveness so that they could fight bulls. When these violent sports were banned, the breed almost disappeared. Later, it was brought back in a more docile form.

## Legendary watchdogs

In ancient times there lived a dog with a truly terrifying appearance: the Tibetan mastiff. This dog, whose strength was matched only by its ferocity, gave birth to today's large mountain dogs, and to the mastiffs. These dogs have inherited the impressive stature of their Tibetan ancestors, and most of them still fulfil protective duties. Like the famous Saint Bernard, the big mountain dogs

The Saint Bernard's cask has saved countless lives... as legend would have it.

The boxer's build, from the front and in profile, is reminiscent of the mastiff: a bulging head, short nose, long thick lips and a sturdy body.

The bull mastiff's hour of glory was in the reign of Richard the Lionheart, who was particularly fond of these guard dogs and fighting dogs.

In China, the Shar-Pei was used in the past to guard temples.

are good-natured, easy-going dogs that show real devotion to humans.

## Short and powerful jaws for vicious dogs

The mastiff group of big dogs is directly descended from ancient fighting dogs, which in turn are the descendants of the Tibetan mastiff. They are thick-set animals – apart from the German mastiff – and often have shortened upper jaws to give them a more powerful bite. Whether the breed is ancient –

like the 2000-year-old Neapolitan mastiff – or more recent, like the boxer or the pit bull, these animals make fearsome guard dogs.

## Dogs of the frozen north

The far North and the far East are the homes of the nordic and spitz dog families. The appearance and character of these dogs closely resemble those of wolves. They make  loyal and resilient servants, and have been used by

The Staffordshire bull terrier was renowned in the fighting pits.

The Spitz, which originated in Germany, is a descendant of the 'peat-bog dog' that lived 6000 years ago. It is highly valued for its thick fur and cheerful yapping.

The German mastiff is a popular choice of guard dog. A rather calm dog, its imposing size is enough to dissuade strangers from entering its territory.

Siberian huskies move with astonishing ease over the thick mantle of snow in the frozen north, where hoofed animals find their hooves a handicap.

The samoyed owes its fame to the explorer Robert Scott.

humans to fill many different roles: sled dog, hunting dog, guard dog…

## The Alaskan malamute, king of the sled dogs

Malamutes are tireless sled dogs, outrunning all their competitors over long distances. These big dogs, well suited to the rigours of life in the frozen north, cannot stand heat or city life. Besides, it is absolutely essential to channel their acute sense of hierarchy in order to prevent aggressive outbursts.

## The akita, revered by the Japanese

Like all dogs in the spitz family, akitas have tails that roll over on to their backs, and are rather smaller than huskies. The Japanese have long valued their forceful temperament and strength, and used them for hunting, guarding against bears, and for dog fights.

Dog lovers tend to prefer blue-eyed huskies.

The akita, originating from the province of the same name, has become the object of a cult in Japan. The city of Tokyo even dedicated a monument to the dog!

The pointer is a champion gun dog, and also makes a skilful retriever. Pointers prefer dry plains to marshland, since their smooth coats offer little protection against the elements.

# The world of hunting dogs

Hunters began to enlist the aid of dogs in the very distant past: cave paintings dating from 4000 BC show dogs accompanying people on hunts. Over the ages three main types of hunting dog have been bred: hounds, gun dogs and terriers.

The Hamiltonstövare, named after its Swedish breeder, is used especially for hunting deer and wild boar.

When dogs were domesticated they lost none of their prodigious hunting abilities. Their most important features in this respect are their keen sense of smell and exceptional stamina for long runs. In the beginning, people bred races of hound that could hunt other animals, running after their prey in a barking pack. Later, with the introduction of firearms, hunters began to breed gun dogs: dogs that work alone, searching for game to flush out. In addition, a third type of hunting evolved: driving the animals out of their holes with small dogs such as dachshunds and terriers.

The Saint Hubert breed was perfected by monks in the Ardennes.

## The bleu de Gascogne, a stolid hound

The grand bleu de Gascogne occupies a special place among the many French breeds of hound. It is believed to be descended from the legendary Saint Hubert, which would make it the ancestor of the best-known breeds. Its 'creator' Gaston Phébus comte de Foix, author of the 14th-century *Livre de la chasse*, developed the breed to hunt hares and deer. Their fine sense of smell

The sturdy grand bleu de Gascogne has a deep, powerful bark that it lets loose while tracking its prey. It is not the quickest of dogs, but was nevertheless used to hunt wolves.

▼ In Europe, hunting has long been a privilege granted to noblemen and women. In the Middle Ages and the following centuries, the nobility kept packs of hounds in order to enjoy this 'pastime'. They bred their own dogs, each one favouring a particular type according to the kind of game they hunted, and the different ideas of beauty that were in vogue in each region and each period. With the decline of hunting with hounds, several of these specific breeds came close to disappearing.

The tough coat of the griffon fauve de Bretagne allows it to go through thick thorn bushes without worrying about painful scratches.

and powerful bark make them highly appreciated pack dogs.

## Hunters and starlets fight over basset hounds

Despite its small stature, around 35 centimetres at the shoulder, the basset hound is used for hunting hare, rabbit, deer and even wild boar. The history of the breed begins in France, with the basset Artesian Normand, then moves on to England, and finally to America, where several breeders imported them and were

The basset hound enjoys country breaks as much as city luxuries.

charmed by their gentle nature and clumsy appearance. Basset hounds have come a long way from the excitement of the traditional hunt, where they enjoyed sprawling in brambles and wallowing in mud. Now they content themselves with lolling on cushions; some even eat at the best American restaurants.

## The 'cataleptic' performance of the pointer

Today's pointers are the undisputed top gun dogs. They

The beagle was Queen Elizabeth I's favourite dog.

The griffon vendéen has a lively and impulsive character that leads it to start off too quickly after game. They sometimes get out of breath and have to give up over-ambitious pursuits.

The family tree of the Hungarian pointer has many branches. Its most important ancestors are the Hungarian hound and the Turkish yellow hunting dog.

The profusion of breeds of gun dog can be largely explained by the growing popularity of hunting and the use of firearms. As well as pointers, this group includes several other breeds that can be classed according to their coats and their preferences for particular types of game. The sturdy smooth-haired pointers and the hardy coarse-haired griffons are versatile hunters; while the long-haired spaniels and long, wavy-haired setters prefer to hunt feathered game.

Few dogs can rival the English springer spaniel when it comes to flushing game.

probably originated when a breed of Spanish pointer arrived in Britain in the 18th century, and was then crossed with French and Italian breeds. The pointer moves swiftly over the leafy plain, its preferred hunting ground, with its nose in the air in search of game of the furred or feathered variety. As soon as it has detected its prey it displays the most spectacular example of pointing in the canine world: it freezes on the spot, as if paralysed.

## The cocker spaniel, the woodcock hunter

Beneath its sophisticated appearance, the cocker is a hardy hunter. It has a fine sense of smell, inherited from its ancestors in the spaniel family; and its British breeding has forged a cheerful and wily character. Hunting woodcock, the cocker stops and points briefly, and then after the shot has been fired it rushes through thickets and bushes to the game, which it carries back with an extremely delicate touch. With their thick coats, cockers are quite at home in marshland, where they pursue waterfowl with great cunning and relish.

## The shipwreck survivors

In 1807 a brig flying the British flag was wrecked off the coast of Maryland, USA. Two Newfoundland terrier puppies were saved and taken in by people who then crossed them with local retrievers. Their descendant is the famous Chesapeake Bay retriever. This large dog, with its oily waterproof coat, thinks nothing of diving into icy waters to retrieve game.

The golden retriever, a very sociable dog, is a children's favourite.

Beneath the brown coat of the Chesapeake Bay retriever is a thick woolly lining. They are so well insulated that they make light of harsh winters and are not afraid of icy water.

Because of its silky coat, the cocker spaniel is more often found in living rooms rather than running across fields. But without sufficient exercise, cockers quickly become overweight.

After tracking otters, the Airedale terrier now hunts criminals.

## The dachshund, the underground worker

Todays dachshunds are often found in the smartest drawing rooms, but in Britain and Germany many of them still fulfil their original function: hunting animals in their burrows. The rough-haired dachshund is particularly suited to this type of hunting; thanks to its thick coat, it does not mind thorns or the cold. Fearless, dachshunds harry foxes, badgers and otters to the bottom of their holes, which they enlarge with their little paws.

The dachshund makes the most of its long thin shape to rush to the bottom of the warren to bring rabbits back to its keeper, wagging its tail.

The Bedlington terrier was used for a long time to kill rats in mines. It is a curious looking little dog, probably related to the whippet.

## The Airedale terrier, the workers' dog

The River Aire, which runs through Leeds, has given its name to a rat catcher: the Airedale terrier. The breed was created in the 19th century by the industrial workers of Leeds, who could no longer bear to share their lives with rats. These loveable dogs proved to be merciless rodent killers, and once the rats had been exterminated, they were used for hunting otters.

The Yorkshire terrier was originally bred by workers in the wool industry.

Pekinese dogs appear on bronze statues around 4000 years old, and they are as popular today with luxury dog lovers.

# Hounds and lapdogs

*The hound's morphology makes it an exception in the canine world. By turns sheepdogs, guard dogs and gun dogs, hounds are as diverse as many lapdogs. From the smallest to the strangest, they all have their charms depending on the prevailing trends.*

The deerhound hunted deer and stags on its home territory, alongside the Scottish nobility.

The fierce wolfhound helped to eradicate the wolf in Ireland.

**B**ecause of the hound's very ancient origins, the places and the various stages of its selection are somewhat uncertain. However, this sharp and lean dog may have originated in Ethiopia and rapidly spread into Asia and Europe via Egypt, while some say that another stock originated in the French region of Brittany. The hound was bred for hunting and successfully pursues hares using only its sight and a speed that

The small Italian hound's size and delicate appearance made it a great hit with many kings and queens, including Cleopatra and Francois I.

The Ibizan hound, which is similar to the Pharaoh hound, is a very capable rabbit hunter due to its well-developed sense of smell and its speed.

The whippet, which is a miniature replica of the greyhound, can reach speeds of 65 km/h.

is very close to 60 kilometres per hour.

## A Vestige Conserved in the Balearic Islands

The Phoenicians helped to export hounds from Egypt through their commercial voyages. The specimens sold in the Balearic Islands at the time had not been crossed with other dogs, and, because of the archipelago's isolation throughout the centuries, the breed remained pure until modern times in the shape of the Pharaoh hound. The dog, which is atypical due to its high-set ears, is an enthusiastic and fast hunter and is also a very popular pet because of its cheerful temperament.

## The Noah's Ark Hound

The Afghan hound, whose history is lost in the mists of time, may have been sheltered on Noah's Ark during the Deluge. However, it is most certainly the

The long-haired Afghan hound is smaller than the short-haired Afghan.

The greyhound took on its present shape under the reign of Henry VIII. At that time, this hound was used to chase hare, because of its speed.

The Borzoi was bred by a Russian noble exiled by Ivan the Terrible, and almost became extinct during the Russian revolution.

The Maltese toy dog is often treated like a live plaything. Their fashion-conscious owners adorn them with 'jewels'.

haughty allure of the dog, rather than this legend, which has led to its great success. The high mountain Afghan, used for hunting, but also to guard flocks, is the most well-known variety. It can be distinguished from other Afghans by its very long and extraordinarily thick coat, which is probably the result of crossbreeding with sheepdogs.

## The Lapdog

Breeds of dogs come in a variety of different

The French bulldog is smaller than its English cousin, and gentler.

sizes: while the largest run through the countryside guarding flocks and hunting game, the smallest stroll through urban streets. These small and sometimes very elegant animals which alleviate human loneliness, act as toy dogs and as confidants are lapdogs.

## A Charming Companion since Antiquity

Dogs related to toy dogs already existed in Ancient Egypt, during the reign

The toy dog is a picture of elegance, with a bow in its hair or under a daffodil.

Legend has it that the Pekinese may be descended from the lion and a monkey, and thus inherited the noble and proud demeanour of the former, and the gentleness and liveliness of the latter.

The Cairn terrier was used in Scotland for fox hunting in the 'cairns' (fissures in rocks). These days, it is a very popular pet.

of Ramses II. In the first century BC, the Greek geographer Strabon described these very same dogs, which were found then on the Island of Malta in the middle of the Mediterranean. It is very likely that the Maltese toy dog that we know today is directly descended from these dogs with this very prestigious past.

## The Dalmatian's Elegant Markings

 As the favourite dog of the 19th century English

In the 15th century, the Brussels griffon was already posing for paintings.

By custom, every fire brigade in the US has its own dalmatian, but the mascot is very often substituted with a canine effigy.

The poodle left the marshes when King Louis XV opened his doors to it. In the 19th century, fashion dictated that the poodle become a small perfumed lion.

dandies, the dalmatian was one of the indispensable accessories that all gentlemen had to be seen to sport in public. At that time, the English called dalmatians 'coach dogs' because it was common practice to have a dalmatian follow when travelling in a luxurious barouche. During the same period, the dalmatian was enjoying similar attention on the other side of the Atlantic; in the Southern states of the US rich plantation owners had to keep one as a symbol of success.

The Yorkshire terrier, with a pretty red bow, is admitted to shows.

The chihuahua can pride itself on being the valued descendant of a pre-Columbian dog called the techichi. The breed was then developed in the US.

# Part two

# Dogs
# in
# OurWorld

In the 16th century, Henri II (1519–59), king of France (1547–59), liked to see his mistress, Diane de Poitiers, depicted as Diana, the Roman goddess of hunting.

# From the earth to the starry sky

*Dogs are omnipresent in human life, and it is only natural that they feature in the fantastic tales that people tell. Although they are sometimes despised, they still fill important roles, like the terrible Cerberus, guarding the centre of the Earth, or Sirius the hunter, which became a constellation.*

At Luxor, as at other Ancient Egyptian sites, the princes' tombs are decorated with frescos depicting embalming scenes.

The dog is humanity's oldest and most faithful companion, and will follow its keeper anywhere, in any circumstances. This mutual attachment has inspired many myths, particularly those in which humans are guided into the next world by dogs.

## Xolotl, the Aztec god-dog

In the Aztec pantheon, which is a mixture of divinities from the Mayan and Toltec civilisations, a

Terracotta dog figurine, excavated at Colima (Aztec territory).

In the pre-Columbian city of Teotihuacán, the ceremonial structure was made up of the Pyramids of the Sun and of the Moon.

The dog-headed god Xolotl is rarely found on Aztec monuments. The tongues coming out of his mouth represent the growls of the guardian of hell.

god appeared with the head of a dog. This god, Xolotl, was invoked in times of great drought, and was also associated with all the recurrent movements in the Aztec universe. Xolotl and his famous twin brother Quetzalcoatl went down into Mictlan, the land of the dead. There they found the bones of a woman and a man, and poured their own blood on them. This act brought the two bodies back to life, and a new humanity was born. Since then, Xolotl accompanies the dead, helping

For the Toltec civilization, Quetzalcóatl was the god of creation.

At Luxor, the tomb of Siptah has an unusual fresco showing one Anubis with a dog (or jackal's) body and another with a human body.

Most interpretations of Egyptian mythology mention a god with the head of a jackal when they come to the episodes involving Anubis. Indeed, the physiognomy of that slim, tapering head with its ears sticking up is closer to a jackal than a dog. According to recent studies, however, there may have been no jackals in Egypt at that time; so it is possible, to consider Anubis as a representation of the Pharaoh's dog, a greyhound whose existence in ancient Egypt is confirmed by paintings.

Anubis with Osiris and Horus, the falcon-god.

them to cross the nine rivers along the road to Mictlan.

## Anubis, the embalmer-dog of Egypt

The Egyptian gods readily took on the form of wild or domestic animals, especially in the case of Anubis, god of thieves and the dead. Anubis is either shown with the body of a man and the head of a dog, with a long nose and erect ears, or entirely as a wild dog. His black colouring is the same as that of the sacred resin used by embalmers, and it was Anubis himself who embalmed the body of Osiris after he had been assassinated by Seth, the father of Anubis. After that tragic day Anubis retained his role, faithfully guiding the souls of the dead on their journey to await their final judgement at the throne of Osiris. In Ancient Egypt, whenever there was a death in a family, they invoked Anubis to preside over the funeral rites and the mummification. The family entrusted the dog-god with the responsibility of accompanying the dead person's heart, the seat of their conscience, to be weighed against the feather of the goddess Ma'at.

Avenged on Seth by his son Horus, the falcon-god of the sky, Osiris, the god of the underworld, is faithfully assisted by Anubis.

## Cerberus, the master of the underworld

The kingdom of Hades, the underworld of Ancient Greece, is guarded by Cerberus, a monstrous three-headed dog. Sometimes he is depicted with even more hideous features: a dragon's tail, serpents' heads darting from his back, and black venomous fangs. The souls of the damned who enter the kingdom of Hades are welcomed warmly by Cerberus, but

Anubis and Hathor, the goddess of love and fertility.

if they try to escape their destiny he devours them with savage cruelty. Nevertheless, Hercules, a man from the world of the living, succeeds in returning from the kingdom of Hades. For his twelfth labour, the hero goes down to the gates of the underworld, provokes Cerberus into a fight, defeats him and puts him in chains.

## Dogs in the sky

In Greek mythology, which is full of surprising twists and

Only the animal parts of the Egyptian god Anubis were black, the colour of the sacred embalming resin.

As part of his final task, Heracles (also known as Hercules) brings Cerberus from the underworld to Eurystheus, the King of Mycenae, who imposed the twelve Labours.

Greek pottery was often decorated with black ink. This scene shows a hunter and his dog, like Orion and Sirius, as they set out to go hunting.

Many classical painters, including Louis de Boulogne the Younger, were inspired by mythology. The sleeping goddess Diana was an extremely popular subject.

turns, Artemis, the goddess of the hunt, was beset by a host of suitors. They were burning with desire for the virgin goddess and one of them, the hunter Orion, even tried to carry her off. Unfortunately for him, Artemis was a fierce defender of her virtue. She produced a scorpion which killed Orion and his faithful dog Sirius. The jilted lover and his dog were turned into stars, and since that time they have made up the constellations of Orion and Canis Major.

Artemis, the hunting goddess sends her dogs in pursuit of deer.

Despite unwavering devotion to his master Tintin, Snowy is sometimes unable to resist temptation. A drop of whisky and the devil in him gets the better of his guardian angel.

The Chinese ideogram that signifies the dog includes the stem that expresses ferocity.

## The Chinese sign of the dog

Chinese astrologers studied the movements of the stars in the sky and developed a horoscope based on the lunar calendar. The horoscope consists of twelve signs representing the twelve animals that answered the call of the Jade Emperor. People born in a year of the dog (1994, 1982, 1970, 1958, 1946, 1934) are believed to have a loyal and honest character.

## An unclean animal

The dog does not always enjoy the privileged position of being man's best friend. In a Tatar legend it was a dog, corrupted by the devil, that was responsible for the downfall of humanity. The Yakuts and the Buryats likewise have little regard for the animal they believe to be cursed by God. In the world of Islam the dog is praised for its loyalty, but its good name is sullied by several Satanic characteristics.

In his version of *Paradise*, Lucas I Cranach (1472–1553) depicted Eve with a sleeping greyhound at her feet.

In 1994, the Hong Kong Royal Mail issued a set of stamps celebrating the year of the dog.

Fables use animals to personify human shortcomings. The well-fed dog symbolizes security, while the hungry wolf represents freedom.

# Stories and legends about dogs

*Humans' stories are linked to those of their family pets, and dogs play a particularly prominent role in this respect. They have achieved immortality alongside their owners in volumes crammed with legends that present them all as heroes.*

The hunter Actaeon accidentally came upon the goddess Artemis as she was bathing. Artemis transformed him into a stag and, in a cruel act of fate, he was torn to pieces by his own hounds.

Alexander the Great gave the name of his favourite dog, Peritas, to a city.

F ollowing the example of the common people, the great names of Antiquity appreciated the company of dogs, and the stories of their exploits make reference to the faithful four-legged friends who accompanied them on all their adventures.

## Alexander the Great's menagerie

Astride his war horse Bucephalus, in the fourth century BC Alexander the Great

On this sculpted low-relief dating from the 5th century BC, a dying man spends his last moments in the company of his son, his wife and his dog.

Returning from a journey, Pliny the Elder (23–79 AD) described a group of islands off the coast of Africa. The islands were inhabited by dogs and became known as the 'Canaries'.

In Pakistan, cruel traditional animal fights still take place.

conquered a vast territory stretching from Macedonia to the banks of the Indus. Historians tell of the time when Alexander was given an enormous dog by the King of Albania when passing through the country. To test the animal's bravery, Alexander set it against bears, wild boar and deer. Because of the dog's passivity the young emperor ordered it to be killed immediately. The King of Albania then offered him his last hound and suggested that his guest pit the dog against animals worthy of combat. The second dog defeated a lion and then an elephant, and was finally accepted by Alexander. Plutarch also refers to the emperor's affection for dogs in the Life of Alexander, stating that when Peritas, Alexander's favourite dog, died, the emperor built a city which bore the animal's name.

## Argos Finds his Master

In the Odyssey, Homer describes Ulysses, King of Ithaca's long voyage, from his departure for the Trojan Wars to his return to his island. While Ulysses was drifting from adventure to adventure, young princes were courting his wife Penelope. After twenty years without news, it was rumoured at the Ithacan court that King Ulysses has disappeared. Unrecognizable, aged and exhausted, he had nevertheless managed to find the shores of his island where he wandered in complete anonymity. Only his faithful dog Argos recognized him, despite the fact that his eyesight was failing due to age. The old dog wagged his tail to greet his master and suddenly tears of emotion filled the valiant warrior's eyes. The completely faithful Argos

Homer's *Odyssey* still continues to influence western culture today.

On his return to Ithaca, Ulysses (Odysseus) was immediately recognised by his dog. He was also recognised by his nurse, Eurycleia, whom he ordered to keep his identity secret.

▼ Many Medieval European fables describe the nobility's favourite animals and praise their characteristics. The knights of the era appreciated the company of the hound, which symbolized faithfulness, an essential aristocratic virtue. For this reason, images of the dogs are found on tapestries, coats of arms and at the feet of their owners on tombs. In Greenland, the Inuit have a similar custom: they place a dog's head beside a dead child.

finally died of exhaustion when King Ulysses went to join the courtiers coveting his estate…

## The Canine Delegation to Jupiter

Phaedra, a Latin fable writer and contemporary of Christ, explains why dogs sniff each other's behinds when they meet. Harshly treated by their masters and unhappy about having to find their food in rubbish bins, the dogs met and decided to send a delegation to plead

In spite of his age, Argus came to greet his master Ulysses on his long-awaited return.

The canine trait of sniffing, which enables a dog to identify another dog by the smell given off from its anus, is the subject of Phaedra's humorous fable.

Jupiter, the chief ancient Roman deity was the sky god, bringer of light and god of thunder and lightning, enough to inspire awe into a delegation of disgruntled dogs.

their case before Jupiter. However, the delegates dallied on the way, which irritated the king of the gods; he was annoyed by their lateness, and became angry when they arrived. The terrified dogs loosened their sphincters and excreted in the reception room. On Earth, the gathering of dogs was told of the incident and feverishly began to form a second delegation: 'Fearing another accident of a similar nature, the dogs' orifices were plugged with half-burnt pieces of perfume.' However, Jupiter

Mosaic of a dog on the threshold of a house in Pompeii, near Naples.

Throughout the Roman Empire, villas were decorated with mosaics. This scene shows hunters returning from hunting hare with their greyhounds.

Illustration of the tale of *The Donkey and the Dog*, by Jean de la Fontaine.

greeted the new delegation with a loud thunderbolt, which so frightened the dogs that they dropped the plugs and made the same mess as the previous group. Phaedra concludes: 'As they are awaiting the second delegation, a dog who sees a newcomer approach sniffs the place where the perfume should be.'

## The hound of Culann the blacksmith

The Celtic legends of Táin Bo Cuailnge

In La Fontaine's fable, *The Man and the Flea*, a man invokes Jupiter to help him get rid of a flea. The dog that was the carrier of the parasite is reminiscent of Phaedra's discontented curs.

UNE CATASTROPHE EVITÉE GRACE AU FLAIR D'UN CHIEN

Dogs are also sometimes the heroes of every-day events which make for gripping stories.

(The Cattle Raid of Cooley), written at the beginning of the eighth century, tell of the adventures of Cúchulainn and other Irish heroes. Part of the story takes place in the court of King Conchubair. Culann the blacksmith invites the king and Setanta his adopted son to his celebrations. Setanta is playing and promises his father that he will join him later, but Conchubair is distracted by the festivities and forgets to warn Culann that his son

Dogs feature in the illustrations of a 10th-century religious book from Catalonia that tells the story of Noah's Ark. They are similar in appearance to the hounds of Eivissa (Balearic Islands).

Handle of 4th-century BC bronze pitcher in the shape of a dog, Celtic art often drew inspiration from animals.

Statues in Las Palmas, attest to the importance of dogs in the islands' history.

will be late. When the young Setanta arrives he is attacked by the blacksmith's guard dog, which has been left unattended. The boy, who already possesses amazing strength, kills the animal with his bare hands, and to make amends for his wrongdoing, Setanta immediately suggests to Culann that he take the lost dog's place for the time being. The druid Cathbad takes the opportunity to rename Setanta 'Cúchulainn', which means 'the Hound of Culann'.

An unexpected result of anthropocentrism: the dog starts imitating its master's behaviour!

# The dog at the service of humanity

*Humans do not seek out the company of dogs so much for the affection they give as for the services that they can perform. As well as helping to conquer the poles and space, everyone's best friend also enlivens the circus ring and assists disabled people.*

Troops being helicoptered onto the high, snow-covered plateaux of Kazakhstan. Able to withstand the harshest climate, the dog often comes to the rescue of humans.

W hen humans beings decided to domesticate the wolf, it was most certainly not to create a pet, but rather to have the wolf work alongside them.

## The ancestral occupations

One of the first tasks dogs performed for their owners was defence. In fact, even when domesticated, the dog,  being a predator, tends to defend its territory, and only tolerates the

The company of dogs is also a great comfort in group therapy sessions.

Fox hunting is renowned for its elegantly dressed riders, courageous horses and packs of noisy, mettlesome foxhounds.

Training a sheep dog requires a close relationship between the shepherd and the dog.

Numerous precautions are necessary when training a guard dog.

presence of its keeper. Used to chasing intruders away, the dog transferred its skills to guarding flocks. Being a gifted partner, the dog very quickly began to accompany its owner when hunting, before becoming its owner's best friend.

## Dogs in the Arena

The Romans, who were very fond of cruel and bloody spectacles, loved to pit their ferocious dogs against tigers,

In the 19th century, it was customary for mastiffs to wear a studded collar and for their ears to be cut to a point to make them look more menacing.

lions and bears. During the Middle Ages, this practice was widespread throughout Europe, although it varied somewhat from place to place. For instance, in Great Britain bulldogs were specially bred to fight bulls in the very popular sport of 'bull-baiting'. In 1689, the Dutch were the first to outlaw this unwholesome entertainment which led to it being banned worldwide, even though clandestine fights still take place today.

Unfortunately, dogs are still trained for fighting.

The Romans built huge structures where they put on entertainments and games. The huge Coliseum in Rome could easily accommodate 50,000 spectators.

## Racing Dogs

Thanks to their athletic qualities of speed and endurance, dogs have also played a part in the human passion for racing. In Great Britain and the US in particular, fast dogs, often greyhounds, are raced against each other on a sandy track while chasing a decoy. These spectacular races are as exciting as horseracing and betting takes place. In Alaska, Siberia and

Aroused by the thrill of the chase, these greyhounds are pursuing decoys.

Shaggy Afghan hounds do not look as powerful as greyhounds because their long hair flies in the wind when they run.

Originally confined to the lands of the Frozen North, teams of dogs pulling sleds are now found in all snow-covered regions.

In 1913, the Belgian army used dogs to pull machine guns.

Greenland, other types of dog races have a more slippery appeal: in these snowy countries, teams of dogs, driven by their mushers, compete, pulling sleds for distances of sometimes more than 1000 kilometres.

## Unwilling Foot Soldier

Humans decided to use dogs to support them at war: soldiers in the Greek, Roman, Gaulish, and Persian armies frequently entered the battlefield accompanied by ferocious dogs that they set upon enemy ranks. A subtle variation on this, used by the Egyptians and Gauls in particular, and later in Medieval Europe, was to cover the dog with sharp metal spikes in order to lacerate the hooves of the enemies' horses. It is also said that King  Henry VIII attacked the army of Emperor Charles V with around 500 mastiffs.

At political summits, guard dogs also help provide security.

In the army, dog-loving platoons have the job of training the dogs used for guard duty and tracking.

Charles V, Holy Roman Emperor, was continually at war with François I, king of France, and Henry VIII, king of England who posed a threat to the 'empire over which the sun never set'.

Customs officers at Bogota airport use dogs to sniff suspicious packages.

## A Keen Bloodhound

The world's police and security services use dogs' guarding and defence skills to track down and immobilize criminals. Police dogs must go through a long and rigorous training process in order to be able to chase a fugitive on its handler's orders, and to be able to stop, but not maul, a criminal. Dogs also  possess a quality that makes them suitable for another

Police mine-clearing units use dogs to track the explosives.

job: although detectives are very resourceful they do not possess the dog's keen sense of smell. After painstaking memorization training, dogs can identify the odour of explosives or narcotics, even if the substances are hermetically sealed.

## In the cold of the avalanche

The legend of life-saving dogs began at the Grand-Saint-Bernard hospice in the

Mountain rescue dogs are able to reach the most inaccessible places.

Major earthquakes cause buildings to collapse. Dogs are vital for finding people buried under the rubble.

Alps, where the monks used their dogs to look for people lost in the snow from the 17th century onwards. In the 19th century Barry, the monastery's most famous resident, saved 40 people who were in danger on the mountain. Unfortunately, the 41st person panicked when big friendly Barry ran to meet him covered in snow and barking loudly. The survivor thought he was being attacked by a bear and killed his saviour. In recognition of services rendered, the sorely missed Barry was stuffed and a stele was erected in his honour in the dogs' cemetery in the small French town of Asnières.

Intelligence and patience are the two chief qualities of a guide dog for the blind.

## Helping the blind and the physically disabled

World War I and its many severely injured veterans led to new roles for the dog. Due to the number of people blinded in the war, training schools for guide dogs were set up in Europe and the US to help the wounded in their day-to-day life. Since then, various specialist centres have carried on the task and have refined training

Laitière flamande.

A monument to Barry the mountain rescue dog who saved many lives, in the dog cemetery at Asnières, outside Paris.

Over the centuries, humans have used dogs to perform many different and often unusual tasks. In the 18th century, dogs were used to turn heavy spits, operate blacksmiths' bellows and even pull tradesmen's carts. In Roman times, dogs were a major source of meat for the Gauls. In China, chows were fed on a diet of cereals to enhance the flavour of their meat. The last canine butcher's shops disappeared from Europe in 1925.

methods. If they are specially trained, Labrador retrievers and alsatians can learn to assist physically disabled people by opening and closing doors, picking up a dropped item or calling a lift.

## A circus animal

Tightrope walkers and clowns have also used the  agility and the learning capacity of dogs to perform astonishing acts.

More than a help in the home, the dog is a devoted companion.

Always cheerful and affectionate, the dog is an ideal companion. Trained to help a disabled child, it does its job with enthusiasm and efficiency.

At the end of the 19th century, delicacies were decorated with cut-out pictures. The scenes in these cut-outs were inspired by festive themes, such as the circus.

The pug, Bully, resplendent in fireman's uniform (Berlin, 1925).

However, acrobatics are the domain of small dogs such as the poodle as they are more capable than a large mastiff of balancing on a wire or on a tightrope walker's ball.

## From the laboratory into space

Life sciences research requires in-depth experiments in order to validate or refute theories, and since the 19th century dogs have been widely used in research

laboratories. Thus, against their will, dogs helped French physiologist Claude Bernard to make important discoveries about the liver, while in Russia, Ivan Pavlov carried out successful reflex research thanks to dogs. Although history remembers Yuri Gagarin as the first person in space, it too often forgets Laïka, the dog who made it into space three and a half years before him.

The 19th-century physiologist, Claude Bernard laid the foundations of modern physiology.

Charities select and train dogs to teach them to help the disabled.

On 3 November 1957, Laika boarded Sputnik 2, never to return to earth again. It was not possible to make the return journey in this pioneering era.

The dog in the *Arnolfini Marriage Group* (1434), painted by the Flemish Renaissance master Jan Van Eyck (d.1441), is the symbol of conjugal fidelity.

# Humanity at the service of the dog

*Careful selection of the most suitable breeds has enabled humans to control the destiny of dogs by establishing an inter-dependent relationship. However, although dog-owners expect a great deal from their 'best friend', they also have unbounded admiration for these loyal companions.*

On 15 June 1937, the 'Grand prix d'élégance automobile de Paris' was held in the Bois de Boulogne. This noble mastiff with its two-tone coat is surely the canine equivalent of the Panhard!

Used by hunters to bring back the game, dogs are also very good at baseball ... as long as they're not allowed to bat!

In most industrialized countries, the number of households with dogs is on the increase. As more and more people have experienced the loneliness of city life, attaching ever greater importance to dogs, a serious market has developed.

## The dog lovers' Tables of the Law

The selective breeding of different types of dog, which was initiated by Gaston Phoebus in the

In the Middle Ages, dogs were held in high esteem and featured on manuscripts.

15th century, first developed as an empirical process. Then in the 19th century, spurred on by the newly created dog clubs, breeders took on the idea of strictly defined standards. In April 1873 the British Kennel Club defined the criteria required to meet these standards in its 'stud book'. This movement, which started in England, soon swept across Europe and the rest of the world. In 1911 all the different national dog clubs, with the notable exceptions of

Even in harsh conditions, dogs have the privilege of travelling with their masters.

Originally, the famous poodle cut was designed to make it easier for the animal to swim when it dived into the water in pursuit of a duck.

Cy deuise comment lassemblee se doit faire en este et en yuer.

a quele as
semblee se
fait en telle
maniere
la nuyt de
uant que le
seigneur
de la chase ou le maistre venur
wouldra aler en bois. il doit fai
re venir deuant luy les veneurs
les aydes les vatles et les pages.
et leur doit a chascun assigner
leurs questes en certain lieu. et

separer lun de lautre. et lun ne
doit point venir sus la queste
de lautre ne faire ennuy. et
chascun doit quester en la ma
niere que luy dist son oncle quil
puet. et leur doit assigner le
lieu ou lassemblee sera au plus
aptie de tous et au plus pres
de leurs questes. Et doit estre
le lieu ou lassemblee sera en
vn biau pre bien vert ou il ayt
biaulx arbres tout au tour.
lun loing de lautre. et vne to

In his hunting manual, Gaston Phoebus describes a picnic scene in which he mentions the care that must be given to dogs.

Grooming a Yorkshire terrier requires the same implements as those used in a hairdressing salon: a hairbrush, rollers and a hairdryer.

A small, playful dog livens up a dance.

Great Britain and the United States, came together under the Federation Cynologique Internationale, based in Belgium. Affiliated dog clubs have a dual role: organising competitions and recording exceptional examples of particular breeds in their official registers.

## Crazy about fashion

For dog shows, owners go to great trouble over their dogs' appearance in order to

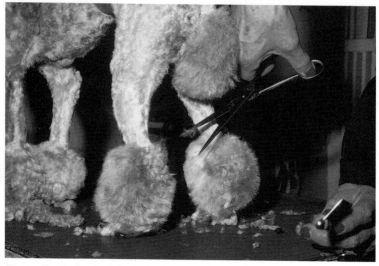
The poodle cut requires great dexterity on the part of the groom to enhance the dog's allure.

In Paris, 70 'caninettes' drive around the streets every day cleaning up dog excrement.

accentuate the features particular to the breed. Inspired by these canine 'top models', the owners of ordinary dogs often wish to treat their own pooches to this kind of grooming and take them to specialist beauty salons. In these salons, professional canine beauticians lavish endless care on their clients. They clean their eyes, ears and teeth, cut their claws and keep their coats in good condition. Dog hairdressers are the undisputed arbiters of canine fashion; in the past, the usual practice was to cut poodles' hair 'lion-style', but now they have imposed the 'crazy' look. In a country like France, with its 2200 beauty salons, all this grooming and beauty care, together with the sales of perfume, dental gel, jackets, ankle boots and dinner suits adds up to an annual turnover of around 400 million francs! Good business indeed, in a constantly growing sector.

Publicity poster for the Chéron veterinary clinic in Paris.

Small breeds are extremely photogenic, adopting poses worthy of movie stars in front of the camera.

## From private clinics

Despite the great care lavished on them by their owners, dogs are no strangers to health problems. 'Town' vets, who often keep up with the most advanced techniques used in human medicine, work wonders to heal sick and injured dogs. Today's specialized veterinary centres use sophisticated diagnostic equipment such as ultrasound and nuclear magnetic resonance (NMR) scanners. Recent advances include the canine pacemaker, which has proven effective in alleviating cardiac deficiencies, chemotherapy and radiotherapy, which have a very good success rate in cancer treatment, and the use of lasers and ultrasound, which can heal lesions in the retina or the crystalline lens. Adherents of alternative medicine, naturally horrified by such traumatizing practices, willingly turn to homeopathy, acupuncture and herbal medicine for their dogs.

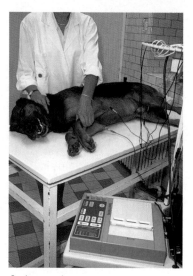

Sophisticated equipment is used for diagnostics.

## ..to dog cemeteries!

Miracle working is not the only prerogative of veterinary

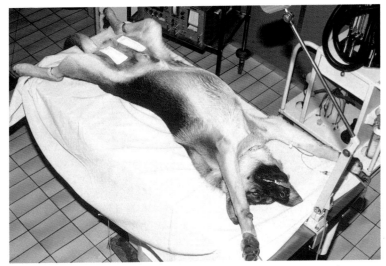

Once the illness has been identified, the vet uses state-of-the-art technology to perform surgery on dogs.

▼ Humanity's devotion to the dog has led some people to go to astonishing lengths for their animals. There are stories, based on eyewitness accounts and ethnologists reports, of women breastfeeding dogs in certain circumstances. This practice has no ritual or mystical significance, it is carried out either to save the life of a poor animal that has no other source of milk, or as a local custom to relieve women who produce too much milk.

Otectomy, or cutting the ears, is a very painful operation.

medicine, dogs suffering from incurable illnesses have to be put to sleep. Their owners, saddened by these brutal losses, can give their dear departed companions a suitable burial in a cemetery for animals. This seems only fair when you consider that in ancient times it was dogs like Anubis and Xolotl who guided humans into the next world. Now it is humanity's turn to provide its most faithful companion with eternal rest.

Like this hound painted at the beginning of the 18th century, François Desportes's portraits were so life-like that they were used in scientific treatises.

When a dog dies, it is hard forget a lifetime of loyalty and affection. In Japan and elsewhere, a tombstone pays a lasting tribute to this faithful companion.

Droopy's sad appearance belies the fact that he is, by his own admission, a happy dog.

## The saga of dogs in art

The first illustrations of dogs, in prehistoric caves, then in the pyramids, come under the heading of religious art. Jan van Eyck gave the dog a new status in art in 1434 when he painted the 'Arnolfi Wedding'. According to art experts, the presence of a lapdog at the couple's feet can be seen as a symbol of conjugal faithfulness, but also of erotic desire. Gradually, dogs became more established in the paintings of the old masters, who appreciated these canine models for their undeniable aesthetic qualities. At the end of the 17th century the painter Alexandre-François Desportes, whose portraits of dogs were highly regarded in England and France, was made official painter of the royal hunts by King Louis XIV.

## The dog as superstar

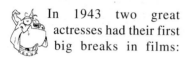 In 1943 two great actresses had their first big breaks in films:

Rantanplan, created by Morris and Goscinny, is the stupidest dog in cartoon history.

In front of the cameras, Lassie embodied the virtues of courage, loyalty and love that made the TV series such an unqualified success. Behind the scenes, she was also an aspiring director!

The American cartoonist Schulz made his character Snoopy into a highly educated dog, full of imagination and confidence and able to rely on his devoted master, Charlie Brown.

Wallace and his dog Gromit live in a world of animated modelling clay.

Elizabeth Taylor, who was ten at the time, and Pal, a collie, starred in *Lassie Come Home*. After Pal's death, no less than three bitches and one dog took over the title role in the endless series of Lassie films. Many others have followed lassie's example, in cartoons such as Walt Disney's *Lady and the Tramp*, and in comic strips such as Snoopy, from the pen of Schulz, and Morris's hilarious blunderer, Rantanplan.

# DOGS
## around the world

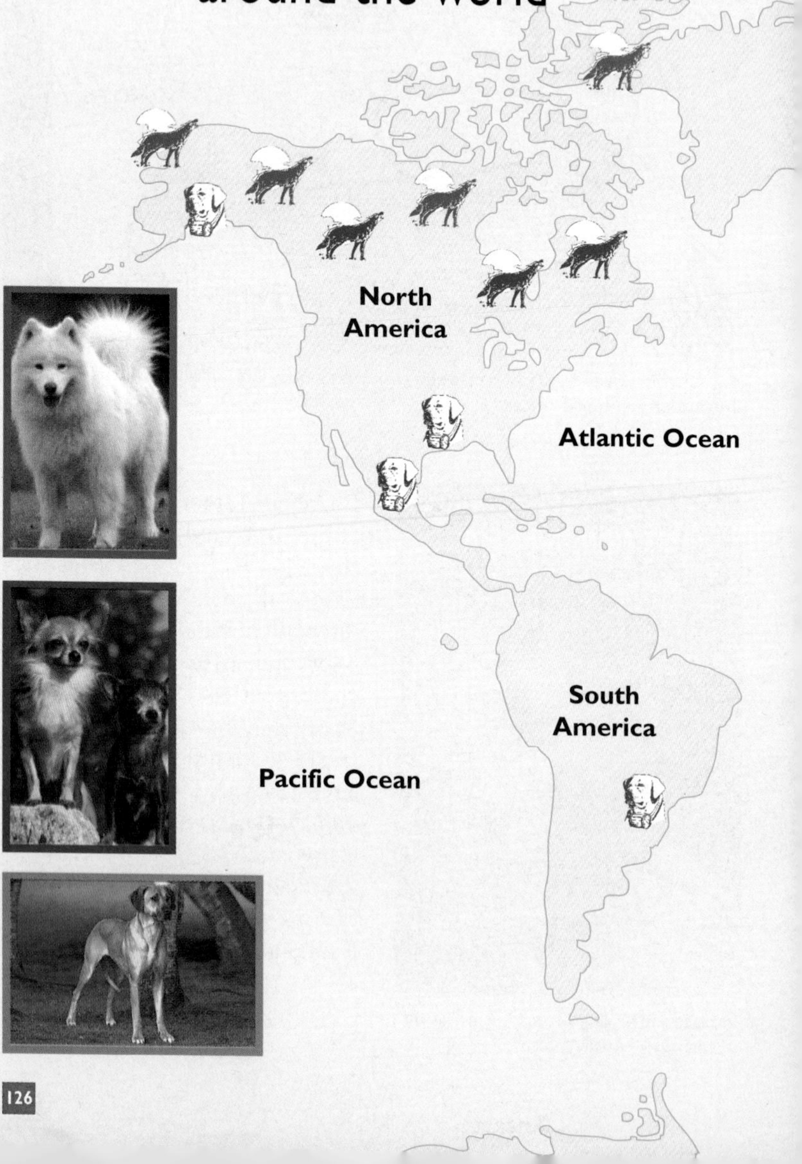

North
America

Atlantic Ocean

South
America

Pacific Ocean

**Arctic**

**Europe**

**Asia**

**Africa**

**Indian Ocean**

**Australia**

| | |
|---|---|
| | **dog** |
| | **wolf** |
| | **jackal** |
| | **dingo** |

**Antarctic**

127

# Dogs

## Principal Species

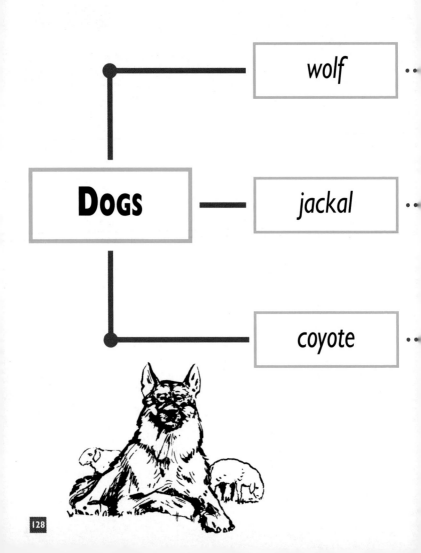

- wolf
- jackal
- coyote

Size, weight and colour of the common wolf (Canis lupus) vary a lot according to his natural environment.

Greyhounds have a wonderfully slender silhouette and a long tapering snout.

The stature of the bulldog is stocky. His frame is huge, his snout short and his outline concave.

The medium-built dingo (Canis lupus familiaris dingo) has escaped human efforts to change its appearance.

During winter time, the coyote (Canis latrans) wears a thick coat, which closely resembles that of a wolf.

Black-backed jackals are characterised by a long dark stripe from neck to tail.

# *Creative workshop*

*Having studied all of these creatures,
it's time to get creative.*

*All you need are a few odds and ends and a
little ingenuity, and you can incorporate
some of the animals we've seen into
beautiful craft objects.*

*These simple projects will give you further
insight into the animal kingdom presented in
the pages of this book.*

*An original and simple way to enjoy
the wonderful images of the animal kingdom.*

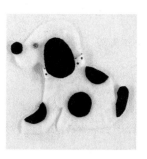

# Dog necklace

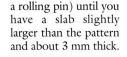

*P*ut your favourite animal on a chain round your neck, with this half-designer, half-ethnic style necklace.

• Photocopy the design and blow it up to the desired size.

↞———— 7 CM ————↠

## Preparing the modelling clay

• Knead the Fimo modelling clay until soft. Roll it out on the sheet of glass with the roller (as if using

a rolling pin) until you have a slab slightly larger than the pattern and about 3 mm thick.

## Cutting out the shape

• Place the photocopy on the slab of modelling clay and press lightly with the palm of the hand so that it stays firmly in place. Cut out the shape with the cutter, cutting through

the paper and the modelling clay at the same time, and remove the excess all round. If the edges are not straight, pat them with the flat of the cutter blade to even them off.

## Decoration

• Take some powdered pigment on the paintbrush and sprinkle it lightly over the top

surface and sides of the dog.

• Place the piece of gold leaf on top and press lightly with the paintbrush to make it stick on.

• Place the two beads where the eyes should be, and push to press them into the modelling clay.

• Using the wooden stick, make a hole in the right ear for the cord to go through.

## Firing

• Place the dog on a sheet of aluminium foil and put it in the oven at 130°C for 25 minutes.

## Finishing

• After it has completely cooled, fix the colours with hairspray or fixative and thread the cord through the hole.

• Take the two ends of the cord together and thread them through the green bead, the golden ring and the blue bead. Make a knot in each of the two lengths of the cord five cm from the last bead, then thread a green bead onto each side.

• Thread the eye of the clasp onto one end and the hook fastening onto the other, then

the two clamping bands to hold the tips of the cord; squeeze them shut with the pliers. Cut off the excess cord so that it ends exactly level with the clamping bands.

## Materials

• White Fimo modelling clay • A cutter.
• A sheet of plate glass or other hard, smooth support to work on • A rubber roller
• A wooden stick (cocktail stick) • Ultramarine pigment in powder form (or acrylic paint of the same colour) • A paintbrush • Two small blue glass beads • A piece of gold leaf if desired • A 50 cm length of blue cord
• A green oval bead, a blue one, a golden ring and two long green beads • A necklace clasp (made up of a ring, a fastening hook and two ring bands for clamping the cord) • A pair of pliers • A can of hair-spray or fixative

# A cushion for the dog

*F*our bones made out of Fimo modelling clay give a touch of humour to this soft and cosy cushion.

• Photocopy the pattern and blow it up to the desired size.

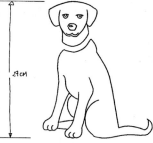

## Making the dog

• Trace the drawing onto the tracing paper and go over the reverse side of the drawing with a lead pencil.
• Place the sheet of tracing paper on the striped cloth and hold it down at the four corners

with the adhesive tape. Make a transfer of the pattern onto the cloth.
• Cut out the striped cloth following the line of your transfer.
• Place this cut-out in the middle of one of the squares of blue cloth and pin it in place.
• Sew the edge of this cut-out onto the blue cloth with the sewing-machine,

using the smallest possible zigzag stitch or bourdon stitch (if your machine does it).
• Place the four studs between the head and the body and stick or sew them on.

## Making the piping

• Place the braid in the

middle of the strip of patterned blue cloth and fold this in half around the braid. Machine-stitch as close to the braid as possible. Place the piping on the right side of the cloth and machine-sew,

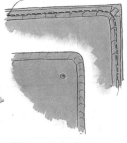

following the first seam. Cut the cloth close to the seam at the corners so as to get the piping to bend round.
• Place the second blue square on top of the first (with the piping on the inside) and sew, leaving a 10 cm gap in the middle of one side.
• Turn the cushion right side out and place an eyelet in each **corner, taking care to make a little hole**

through the two thicknesses of cloth beforehand.

• Fill the cushion with kapok, without stuffing it too full so that the cushion is not too thick, and hand-sew the remaining opening.

## Making the bones

• Take the Fimo and knead it until soft and easy to handle. Make a sausage-shape 40 cm long and 1 cm in diameter and cut four sections 7 cm long out of it.

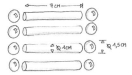

• Make eight balls 1.5 cm in diameter (roll pieces of modelling clay between your palms) and stick them at either end of each of these sections.

• Model the tips into a bone-shape, then place the sections on aluminium foil. Place the foil on a baking tray in an oven heated to 130°C for 25 minutes.

When you remove them from the oven, twist each bone slightly so that it is bent at an angle.

• Wind the cord round each bone and thread the two ends though the eyelet. Fasten in place by tying a knot on the underside of the cushion.

## Materials

• Two 45 cm squares of blue cloth • A 40 cm square of green and white striped cloth
• 2.50 m of patterned blue cloth 4 cm wide • 2.50 m of braid piping • A sheet of tracing paper • Adhesive tape • A lead pencil • A pair of scissors • Pins • A sewing machine • Four round white studs for sticking or sewing on • Super-glue • Kapok to stuff the cushion with
• White Fimo modelling clay • Four no. 4 gold-coloured eyelets • White cord (thin enough for a double thickness to pass through one of these eyelets)

# Frieze for a child's bedroom

*Scampering together two by two, these blue poodles will chase all round a child's bedroom to make a naive-style frieze.*

• Photocopy the pattern and blow it up to the desired size.

## Making the stencil

• Place the photocopy on the sheet of Bristol board and hold it down at the four corners with adhesive tape. Cut round the shape of the photocopy, cutting through both layers at the same time.
• Spray the back of the resulting stencil lightly with the spray-can of glue.
• Draw a faint line with a pencil all along the wall at the desired height and place the stencil just underneath, alternating between dogs tilted upwards and tilted downwards.

## Painting the dogs

• Put some turquoise paint on the stencil brush without adding water and dab it inside the stencil on the front half of the dog. Then take some ultramarine paint and dab in the back half of the dog, blending the two colours into each other by adding a little ultramarine on top of the turquoise. Do the same with the orange of the collar.
• Then use a pencil to draw broad curves under the resulting frieze, each curve being the width of two dogs.

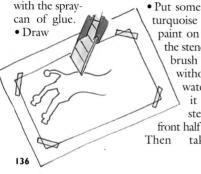

## Making the orange frieze

• Prepare two containers, one for the white and one for the orange.

• Whitewash a broad sweep of the wall, following the curves, then go over them on top in orange using the second brush. The orange will mix with the white, giving you a more subdued colour. Do not make the colour too even, however, as it is the visible brush-strokes that give this colourwash its charm.

• Then take some pure orange paint on the fine paintbrush and paint little fans, freehand, at the intersection of the curves.

## Materials

• An A4 sheet (21 x 29.7 cm) of 250 g Bristol board
• Acrylic paint in ultramarine and turquoise, and white water paint (or emulsion) and orange acrylic for the wall
• A round stencil brush • Two wide brushes for painting the wall
• A fine-tipped paintbrush • Adhesive
• A cutter • A spray-can of glue for mounting

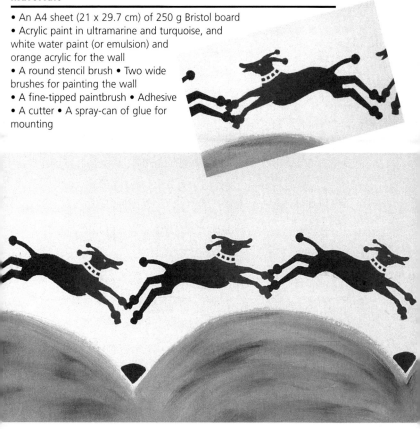

# Dog lamp-shade

*S*ix little Dalmatians in chic black and white do the rounds on this bedside lamp.

### The support

- Measure the lamp-shade, starting from the base and going up to the top circle and down the other side back to the base. Add 10 cm.
- Cut a square of paper for the pattern, making it 5 cm bigger than the distance you have just measured. Fold it in four.
- Using a ruler, measure out half the original distance starting from a corner; mark the paper at regular intervals so as to make a quarter-circle. Cut out the pattern along this arc of

the circle and unfold. Use this pattern to cut a circle out of the cloth.

- Fold the spotted ribbon in two. Slip the raw edge of the cloth between the edges of the folded ribbon. Pin and sew all around the outer edge.

### The dogs

- Draw the dog design onto the pattern paper and use this to cut six of them out of the curtain lining, three facing right and three facing left.
- Cut an ear, a tail, a nose and three round dots 2 cm in diameter out of the lightweight black felt for each dog, together with eight cm of the spotted ribbon.
- Decorate each dog in

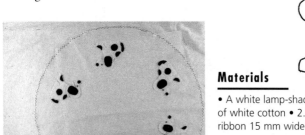

### Materials

- A white lamp-shade • A 60 cm square of white cotton • 2.30 m of spotted ribbon 15 mm wide • Paper for making a pattern • A remnant of white curtain lining • A remnant of lightweight black felt • Adhesive for cloth • Black beads for the eyes.

the same way: fold the ribbon in two and hand-sew it round the dog's neck. Stick on the ear, the tail and the nose and three round dots; for two of these dots, place them so that they are only half stuck down inside the outline of the dog and cut off the excess black cloth from the dots which stick out. Sew on a bead for the eye.

## Assembly

• Stick the dogs five cm from the outer edge, distributing them evenly around the edge and arranging them alternately face to face and back to back.

**Acknowledgements:**

The publishers would like to thank all those who have contributed to this book,
in particular:
Guy-Claude Agboton, Antoine Caron, Jean-Jacques Carreras, Michèle Forest,
Nicolas Lemaire, Hervé Levano, Marie-Bénédicte Majoral, Kha Luan Pham,
Vincent Pompougnac, Marie-Laure Sers-Besson, Emmanuèle Zumstein

Illustration: Frantz Rey

Translation: Kate Clayton - Ros Schwartz Translations, Dave Hallworth, Patricia Clarke

Impression: Eurolitho - Milan
Dépôt légal: September 1998
Printed in Italy